Have You Seen The Notice Board?

(A Few Comments on Realities of Life)

COLLECTED & COMPILED

BY

Brian A Lee-Blackmore

IDEAS UNLIMITED (PUBLISHING)

THE FIRST LAW OF PUBLISHING

IF IT'S OUTRAGEOUS SHIT, BUT WILL MAKE MONEY,
IT'S PUBLISHABLE; BUT IF IT'S PUBLISHABLE,
BUT WON'T MAKE MONEY, IT'S SHIT –
AND THAT'S OUTRAGEOUS.

Published by:
Ideas Unlimited (Publishing)
P.O.Box 125, Portsmouth
Hampshire PO1 4PP

ISBN I 871964 10 5

Illustrations by Willy Sanker

Printed and bound in Great Britain

INTRODUCTION

Arguably, this isn't a collection so much as a selection and might be thought to reflect just one individuals taste. However, judging by the number of engrossed or giggling bodies, congregating around the many notice boards and office walls it's been my privilege to peruse, I'm not alone in thinking that what follows here is funny, pungent or poignant. Humour, though, is subjective and there are those for whom some of these items will not appeal; particularly, I suspect, those pieces which might be considered a touch course or a tad profane and unsophisticated.

Be careful, however, not to condemn too quickly. Consider such items as the product of an imagination that doesn't seek merely to shock, but often contrives to win your attention and make a statement at the likely expense of a few immature sniggers. Certainly, of the few risque examples contained here, none are included if crudeness and vulgarity is the key to their value. The common denominator in all the examples is that, in an indirect way, the authors are trying to convey something very important. The best way is through laughter or amusement, even if the vehicle for that amusement is slightly shocking. While our attention is drawn, we see a range of cold truths made evident by some bright individual perceptive enough to see the flaws in a decision, or yet one more example of shortcomings in the human condition. Somehow, our author is able to distil it all in one picture or pithy statement. Some cynicism must be admitted, but I think this is often an inevitable part of the process of exposing our weaknesses. Sombre, resentful or grim treatments are rare in our authors – they tend to take the lighter side which often has a far greater impact than any serious protest. To expose sham, deceit and exploitation is a concern for the common good, the harshness of an unpalatable truth can sometimes crush any hope of responding to it. To use ridicule is one option for coming to terms with the realities of life.

At times cynicism is expressed openly, the authors speak of disillusionment and searching self-criticism. Whether this kind of thing has any corrective or palliative value must remain a matter of opinion. At the very least, it is a comment on the structure of our society and demonstrates that every walk of life has its own set of grievances. Indeed, I for one, believe this kind of literature to be totally positive, particularly in its ability to keep us tethered to reality. There is a certain humility in such writings which acknowledges the frailties, fears and burdens of even the most sophisticated of people.

Here, then, are a few comments on the realities of life. To the many admirable, but, alas, mostly anonymous authors I offer thanks. As long as people like them survive we, the recipients of their piercing insight, will be allowed to see the truth.

Brian A. Lee-Blackmore

Salisbury 1994

ACKNOWLEDGEMENTS

During the 20 years in which I have been collecting this material, I have never once met anyone who was prepared to claim authorship of a piece of notice board graffiti (at least, no one would openly take credit for having penned the particular piece I was looking at!). You can be sure that I always asked the question, but the individuals modesty always precluded the raising of the quill or admitting any knowledge of the origin of the particular specimen I was looking at. I have no doubt that some veteran 'notice board' authors reading part of this compilation will recognise their own work. I can only excuse my presumption by quoting M. Mizner. Thus:

"If you steal from one author its plagiarism,
If you steal from many, it's research"!

Of course, if you have irrefutable proof that you are the originator of one of these items, I will be more than willing to note it. However, since each epigram, cartoon and missive contained herein is as originally found (grammar, syntax, sentiment, profanities and all) it might be politically unsound – or socially embarrassing – at this late stage to wave the flag. But, if you insist...!

Sincere thanks to those that did show me where to go!
Bob van der Koy. Peter Delbridge. Andy Archibald.
Clyde Brunton. John Halam.
and of course my lovely Mrs B, who tested the metal of the
humour and the plastic of the keyboard.

The 'Everlast' item, by permission from VTECH.

THINK AHEAD

SIX PHASES OF A PROJECT

1. ENTHUSIASM

2. DISILLUSIONMENT

3. PANIC

4. SEARCH FOR THE GUILTY

5. PUNISHMENT OF THE INNOCENT

6. PRAISE & HONOURS FOR THE NON-PARTICIPANTS

O.K. We took off our clothes...
I got on top of you...
How soon before it starts
to feel good?

I don't know, but I already
have a headache.

A TREE IS A PLANT THAT GROWS IN THE SAME SPOT FOR 50 YEARS AND THEN SUDDENLY JUMPS IN FRONT OF A WOMAN DRIVER.

MAN HAS BEEN DEFINED AS THAT WHICH COMES FROM WOMAN AND THEN SPENDS THE REST OF HIS LIFE TRYING TO GET BACK IN.

MONEY CAN'T BUY YOU HAPPINESS – BUT IT MAKES YOUR MISERY A LOT MORE BEARABLE!

"THAT'S THE PROBLEM WITH DIETS – NONE OF THEM REACH ALL THE PARTS THAT DIETS OUGHT TO REACH."

You're not old when your hair is turning to grey,

Or when you're tired at the end of the day,

But you're finished, and you're ready for that long last sleep,

When your mind makes appointments your body can't keep.

Speaking of Life Today is like Talking about Rope in the House of a Hanged Man –
Where will it End?

If you can keep your head when all those about you are losing their's – YOU'RE NOT AWARE OF THE SITUATION!

Claire Raynor,
Breakfast Television,
BBC Television,
LONDON W47 6BN

544326 Murphy P.
H.M. Prison,
Strangeways,
Southall Street,
MANCHESTER

September 27, 1989

Dear Claire,

I am a man aged 24 and come from a large family. My name may be familiar to you as my youngest brother plays football for Bristol City. My older brother is unfortunately serving life in Broadmoor for multiple rape and driving while disqualified. My sisters had their own business, The Erotica Visiting Massage Service, but they gave it up when they realised that they had lesbian tendencies towards one another.

My mother is a mentally retarded alcoholic and refuses to have anything to do with my father since she discovered he is a practising homosexual who has recently contracted aids. She is now pregnant by the Pakistani who owns the off-licence and the doctor says her heroin addition may affect my unborn half-brother.

Whilst inside, I have been writing to a charming girl of my own age, an ex-prostitute with six lovely children, two of them half caste, and we plan to marry when I get out and her syphilis clears up. My problem is, how can I bring myself to tell her about my brother playing for Bristol City?

Yours in Hope,

P. Murphy

DIPLOMACY IS TO DO AND SAY THE NASTIEST THINGS IN THE NICEST WAY

It takes two to make an argument and I think both you bastards are wrong.

AS YOU DECREASE THE LENGTH OF AN ARGUMENT, YOU INCREASE IT'S IMPACT, AND THE MORE IMPACT IT HAS THE MORE LIKELY YOU ARE TO GET INTO AN ARGUMENT.

YOU ARE A LIAR,
I WILL NOT SINK IF YOU
TAKE IT OUT.

MEDICAL AUTHORITIES HAVE ANNOUNCED THAT *AIDS* CAN BE CONTRACTED THROUGH THE *EARS* BY LISTENING TO ASSHOLES

NOAH'S LAMENT

And the Lord said unto Noah "Where is the ark which I have commanded thee to build"?

And Noah said unto the Lord "Verily I have had three carpenters off sick, the Gopher Wood suppliers hath let me down, yea, even though the Gopher Wood hath been on order for, let me see, nigh on 12 months, the damp course specialist hath not turned up and the supplier of Bitumen hath been declared black by the drivers union".

And Jehovah said unto Noah "Hearken unto me Noah, I command thee to finish the ark, even after seven days and seven nights".

And Noah said "It shall be so Lord".

And Lo, after time the Lord said "Why art thou so perplexed Noah"?

And Noah rent his garments saying "The bastard glazier departed to Majorca on Holiday – yea even though I offered him double time."

And the Lord spake unto Noah, saying "And where are the clean beasts that I commanded of thee, the male and the female, to keep their seed alive on the face of all the earth"?

And Noah cried "The van cometh even unto Tuesday, yea and yea it will be so".

And the Lord God Jehovah, causing the heavens to blacken said "speak to me of the unicorns which I commanded of thee".

And Noah wrung his hands and wept sore, saying "Lord, Lord, they are a discontinued line. Thou can'st get unicorns for love nor money".

And Noah kissed the earth and cried "Lord, Lord, thou knowest in thy wisdom what it is like with delivery dates".

And the Lord in his wisdom said "My most beloved son Noah, why else thinkest thou I have only caused a flood to descend upon the earth for forty days and forty nights, thinkest thou it was easy? I planned for twice that!"

(With thanks to the New Zealand Society of Radiographers)

January 15,

Mr Fred Glomph
Sales Manager
Fly-By-Night Gizmo Co.
25 Seedy Street
Cavveat Emtorville

Dear Mr Glomph,

Your "EVERLAST" dining set lasted only 3 days. It disintegrated.

Not only that, but the remains of it dissolved my table, fell on the floor and caused extensive discoloration. And Aunt Maude, while cleaning it up, got some on her hands and immediately fell into a fit. While she was thrashing around on the floor, she kicked our wee son Mortimer in the eye and he, too, is in the hospital. In our rush to take these two casualties to the hospital, my wife left a cigarette burning in the living room and, upon our return, we discovered that our house had burned down. Seeing this and realizing that our insurance had run out, my poor wife, distraught, wandered into the road and she was struck down by a passing bus...number 49, if I recall.

Legal consultation has brought to light the fact that you have covered yourself totally and will assume no responsibility whatsoever for my predicament. Therefore I am sure you will understand fully when I tell you that the paper in this letter has been saturated with Anthrax 46, a fast-acting nerve toxin which has no known antidote. Just touching the paper is enough to give you a lethal dose.

Before the convulsions begin, I hope you will authorize the replacement "EVERLAST" dining set to which I am entitled under your warranty. *After all there is no sense in bearing a grudge.*

Sincerely,

Wadsworth Wort

ORGANISATIONAL CHART

THE BOSS

When the body was first made, all the parts wanted to be Boss. The brain said "I control everything and do the thinking, I should be Boss."

The hand said "since I do all the work which earns the money to keep the rest of you going, I should be the Boss."

The eyes said "I have to look out for all of you and tell you where danger lurks, I should be Boss."

And so it went. The ears, the feet, the lungs and finally the asshole demanded to be Boss. All the parts laughed at this.

The asshole was so enraged that he refused to function. Soon the brain was feverish, the hands hung limply and the eyes crossed. All parts capitulated, and so it happened that all the body parts did the work while the asshole bossed around and passed out lots of shit!

The Moral: You don't have to be a brain to be a Boss, simply as asshole!!

'I'M SORRY SMITH, BUT BEING ABLE TO SKATE AROUND ALL NINE OF THE COMPANIES DEPARTMENTS COMPLETELY BLINDFOLDED DOES QUALIFY YOU FOR SENIOR MANAGEMENT"!

NOTICE

This department requires no physical fitness programme.

Everyone get enough exercise jumping to conclusions, flying off the handle, running down the boss, knifing people in the back, dodging responsibility, pushing their luck and passing the buck.

MATTER OF INTERPRETATION

WHEN I TAKE A LONG TIME -
I'M SLOW.

WHEN MY BOSS TAKES A LONG TIME -
HE'S THOROUGH.

WHEN I DON'T DO IT -
I'M LAZY.

WHEN MY BOSS DOESN'T DO IT -
HE IS TOO BUSY.

WHEN I DO SOMETHING WITHOUT BEING TOLD -
I AM TRYING TO BE SMART.

WHEN MY BOSS DOES THE SAME -
THAT'S INITIATIVE.

WHEN I PLEASE MY BOSS -
THAT IS CREEPING.

WHEN MY BOSS PLEASES HIS BOSS -
HE'S CO-OPERATING.

WHEN I DO GOOD -
MY BOSS NEVER REMEMBERS

WHEN I DO WRONG -
HE NEVER FORGETS!

HOW TO BE LOVED BY YOUR SECRETARY

1. NEVER start work first thing in the morning – we much prefer a terrific rush in the afternoon.

2. Please smoke when dictating: it assist's pronunciation.

3. Do not face us when dictating: this would be too easy for us.

4. Hours for dictating: During the lunch hour or any time between 4.30 and 5.30 p.m.

5. When dictating, please parade up and down the room. We can understand what is said more distinctly.

6. Please call us in for dictation and then proceed to sort out papers, look up old files, telephone and receive calls etc.

7. Please lower the voice to whisper when dictating names of people, places etc. and under no circumstances spell them out to us. We are sure to hit upon the right way of spelling them. We know the name and address of every person, firm and place in the world.

8. When we do not hear a word and dictators are asked to repeat it, shout it as loud as possible. We find this more gentlemanly. Alternatively, dictators should refuse to repeat it at all. We have second sight and it may come to us.

9. Whenever possible, dictators should endeavour to keep us late. We have no homes and are only too thankful for somewhere to spend the evening.

10. Should a letter require slight alteration after it is typed, score the word heavily through about four times and write the correct word beside it, preferably in ink or heavy pencil, and always make the alteration on the top copy.

11. Should we be too busy, or too lazy, to take down dictation, please write letters with a blunt pencil in the left hand, whilst blindfolded. Incorrect spellings, balloons, arrows and other diagrams are very helpful to us.

12. With regard to statements, do not on any account use lined paper. If figures are altered, please write heavily over those previously inserted, the correct figure in each case being the one underneath.

13. Should work be required urgently (a most unusual occurrence) it aids us considerably if you rush in at intervals of 30 seconds to see if it is done.

14. If extra copies of a letter are required, this desire should be indicated either after "Yours faithfully", or overleaf, so as to ensure that it is the last thing the typist see's when the letter is completed.

15. When we stagger out carrying a pile of files, please do not open the door for us; we learn to open it with our teeth, or crawl under it.

GOD I LOVE THIS PLACE...

PLEASE BE PATIENT, I ONLY WORK HERE BECAUSE I AM TOO OLD FOR A PAPER ROUTE, TOO YOUNG FOR SOCIAL SECURITY AND TOO TIRED TO HAVE AN AFFAIR.

NOTICE

MOST EMPLOYEES WILL KNOW THAT OUR PRESENT FACTORY PREMISES GO BACK TO THE 1850'S. RECENT EXTENSION WORK TO THE PLATING SHOP REVEALED AN ALMOST PERFECTLY PRESERVED MACHINE SHOP OF EARLY VINTAGE. A MUMMIFIED WORKER OF THE PERIOD WAS FOUND SLUMPED OVER ONE OF THE MACHINES – APPARENTLY HE DIED OF EXHAUSTION AND THE INHUMAN CONDITIONS PREVAILING AT THE TIME.

VISITS TO THE AREA WILL NOT BE APPROVED – MANAGEMENT BELIEVE STAFF MAY BECOME ENVIOUS AND DISCONTENT WITH THE CURRENT WORKING ENVIRONMENT.

"Those pills you gave me don't seem to be helping much Doctor – it's been two weeks now and I'm the same as if I hadn't taken them."

"On the contrary, if you hadn't taken them you'd be dead by now."

STAFF NOTICE

Management notes that employees dying on the job are failing to fall down.

This practice must cease, it is becoming impossible to distinguish between death and natural movement of staff.

Any employee found dead in an upright position will be dropped from the payroll.

By Order.

C.E.O.

DUE TO THE PRESENT ECONOMIC SITUATION THE LIGHT AT THE END OF THE TUNNEL HAS BEEN TURNED OFF UNTIL FURTHER NOTICE.

THE FLOGGINGS AND HANGINGS WILL CONTINUE UNTIL MORALE IMPROVES

WORK DILIGENTLY, WITH INTEGRITY, AND YOU'LL GET YOUR JUST REWARDS.

SPECIFIC ORGANISATIONAL OPTIONS
BEING LIMITED, AND GIVEN
CURRENT RESTRICTIONS IN
PERFORMANCE MODES,
WE SEE SEVERE RESTRAINTS ON THE
CHOICES AND PROBABILITIES
LIKELY TO CHARACTERISE
RE-ENGAGEMENT OF YOUR
SERVICES – IN SHORT,
YOU'RE FIRED!

**THIS COMPANY PAYS PEANUTS AND
HIRES MONKEYS – GOOD JOB WE'RE
ONLY A MANAGEMENT RECRUITMENT
COMPANY!**

WATCH IT!

THIS IS A BAD DAY. I'M FEELING VERY FRAGILE. SPEAK TO ME QUIETLY IN DULCET TONES AND LET NOT ONE OFFENSIVE WORD BE UTTERED. TAKE CARE TO MOVE SLOWLY (FOR MY VISION IS IMPAIRED AND SUDDEN MOVEMENT MAY ALARM ME). BE AWARE THAT I HAVE OCCUPIED THIS DESK FOR 20 YEARS AND IT PAINS ME TO KNOW THAT HERE I WILL STAY FOR ANOTHER 20 YEARS. TREAD SOFTLY THEN, AND SHOW RESPECT AND REVERENCE FOR SOMEONE OF MATURE YEARS AND GENTLE DISPOSITION – OR I'LL RAM MY PEN UP YOUR ....!

MEMORANDUM

To: All employees
From: Personal Department
Subject: Excessive Absences

Due to the excessive number of absences from the office the following rules and procedures will be put into effect as of this instant.

SICKNESS:

No excuse. We will no longer accept your doctor's statement as proof, as we believe if you are able to go to the doctor you are able to come to work.

DEATH:

(Other than your own) this is no excuse. There is nothing you can do for them and we are sure that someone else with a lesser position can attend to the arrangements. However, if the funeral can be held in the late afternoon, we will be glad to let you off one hour early, providing that your share of the work is ahead enough to keep the job going in your absence.

LEAVE OF ABSENCE:

(For an operation) we are no longer allowing this practice. We wish to discourage any thoughts that you need an operation. We believe as long as you are an employee here, you will need all of whatever you have and you should not consider having anything removed. We hired you as you are and to have anything removed would certainly make you less than we bargained for.

DEATH:

(Your own) this will be accepted as an excuse but we would like a two week notice, as we feel it is your duty to teach someone else your job.

ALSO:

Entirely too much time is being spent in the restroom. In the future we will follow this practice of going in alphabetical order. For instance, those with names beginning with "A" will go from 8.00 to 8.15; "B" will go from 8.15 to 8.30, and so on. If you are unable to go at your appointed time, *it will be necessary to wait until the next day when your time comes again.*

TELL ME IT'S JUST P.M.S. AND I'LL STAPLE YOUR NUTS TO THE FLOOR

ABSENTEEISM

As stated in a previous notice, there has been an alarming increase in absenteeism. The planned address on this subject by the Managing Director has been postponed since he is away at the moment.

GETTING THINGS DONE AROUND HERE IS LIKE MATING ELEPHANTS:-

1. It's always done at high level.
2. It's accomplished with much bellowing.
3. It takes two years to get any results.

I, THE WILLING,

LED BY THE IGNORANT,

AM DOING THE IMPOSSIBLE,

FOR THE UNGRATEFUL.

I HAVE DONE SO MUCH,

FOR SO LONG,

WITH SO LITTLE,

THAT I AM NOW HIGHLY QUALIFIED,

TO DO ANYTHING,

WITH NOTHING!

In any organisation there is always one person that knows precisely whats going on – that little shit must be fired!

Those of you who *think* you know everything are very annoying to those of us who do.

When faced with complete disaster TOTAL defiance is the ONLY answer.

IF YOU ARE UNHAPPY

Once upon a time there was a non-conforming sparrow who decided not to fly south for the winter. Soon the weather turned so cold that he was forced to fly south, in a short time ice began to form on his wings and he fell to earth in a barnyard. Exhausted, almost frozen, he prepared himself for the end. Just then a cow passed by and crapped on the little sparrow. Rather than the quick dispatch which he expected, the sparrow found that the manure warmed him and defrosted his wings. Warm and happy, able to breathe, he started to sing. At that moment, a large cat came by and, hearing the chirping, began to investigate. The cat cleared away the manure, found the bird and promptly ate him.

THE MORAL OF THE STORY

* Everyone that craps on you is not necessarily your enemy.
* Everyone who gets you out of the shit is not necessarily your friend.
* If you're nice and warm and happy in a pile of shit, keep your mouth shut!

WHEN YOU'RE DOWN AND OUT, EVERYONE WANTS TO SCREW YOU.

RIPOFF MOTORS PLC.

NOTICE – WORK COMPLETION.

Should mechanics be asked by customers as to when they expect to complete car repairs, the 'Official Replies List' must be used. The words 'soon', 'X hours, 'now' are prohibited. Permissible replies are 'I don't know', 'When we get the parts' or 'They don't make parts for this anymore'. A sharp intake of breath is allowed under aggressive questioning or extreme duress. It is unfair to customers to have their hopes raised and then to find that the car is actually ready on time. This phenomenon has been carefully researched.

Customers expect to wait at least 72 hours over and above any reasonable time for repairs; early returns can be traumatic. Most of you will know Mr Thomas - we took in his Wolseley 6/110 in 1967 and he tells us that he looks forward to his daily visits here. He amuses us with his tall stories of two occasions when he detected work being done on the car.

There is, of course, a small element amongst the general run of customers who can only be described as difficult. Not only do they create trouble if repairs are over long, but they expect to have repairs done safely and correctly!

Staff should consider this as part of the job and accept that there is little that can be done to remedy it. This kind of attitude is, fortunately, getting rarer.

When, and if, a car is handed back, the customer must sign the Liability Release Form which absolves the company from any responsibility or risk. It is at this time that 'final checks' can be made (out of view of the customer) and 'knock' and 'clunk' modifications can be introduced into the vehicle to ensure the customer comes back. This improves customer contact and gives the recovery truck steady business.

Oxygen and resuscitation equipment is now in operation in the 'Bill Presentation Room'. So far, only two customers have suffered cardiac arrest, following the 100% increase in labour charges, but this is expected to be reduced when the 'Second Mortgage Department' opens in June. The recent bad press that the motor trade has received recently (on the subject of charges) raises the question of accurate recording of overhead costs. From now on, 'customers' vehicles secretly used by the taxi division of our firm, will render the customer liable to charges if said customers vehicle breaks down while in service. Such additional costs (such as compensation for a staff member who misses a weekend at the casino because the customer's car fails to start) will be included in the bill presented to the customer when collecting their car.

Finally, staff are reminded of some 'gratitude' phrases such as: "I worked through the night on this"-, "-sifted for six hours in the scrap yard to find you this part"! and "This is the last time you'll see one of these, but here's my phone number, I might be able to get you one". As a rule, this may mean anything up to 50% on the official bill (now and later) and provides workshop staff with the possibility of alternative income.

N.B The customer, who kidnapped Mr. Roberts our Reception Manager and threatened to dismantle him unless he got his car back, has been told to go ahead.

Signed,
Work Duty Foreman
P.G.Lark.

THE EVOLUTION OF AUTHORITY

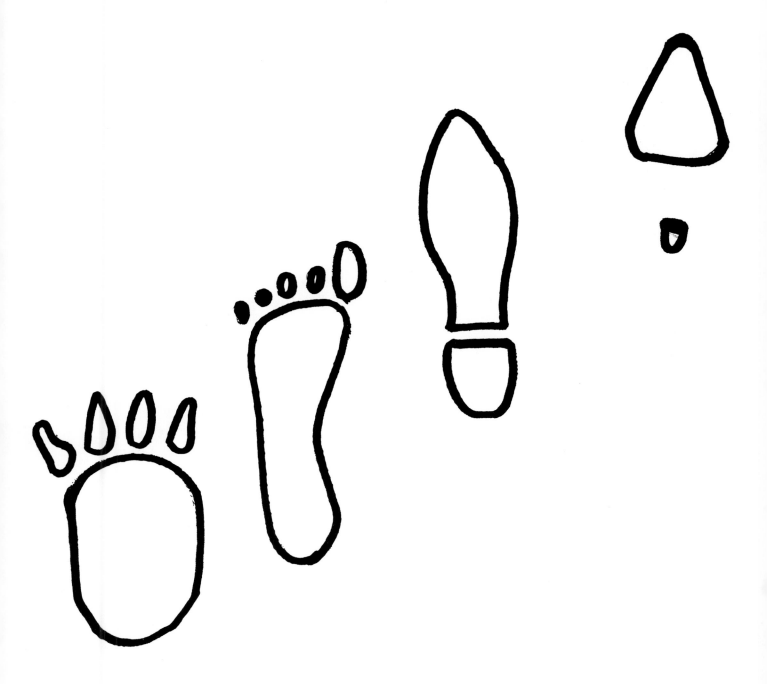

I'm sure you understand what it is you think I said, but I'm not sure you realise that what I said was not what I meant. I intended to make it clear that what I mean to say cannot be misunderstood, and that any misunderstanding is the fault of your own believing that your interpretation of what you thought I said is infallible.

THE ITALIAN
WHO WENT TO DETROIT

(MUST BE READ WITH AN ITALIAN ACCENT)

ONE DAY IMA GONNA DETROIT TO BIGGA HOTEL. INNA MORNING I GO DOWN TO BREAKFAST, I TELLA THE WAITRESS I WANNA TWO PISSESS TOAST SHE BRINGA ME ONLY ONE PISS. I TELLA HER I WANNA TWO PISS. SHE SAY TO GO TO THE TOILET. I SAY YOU NO UNDERSTAND. I WANNA TWO PISS ONNA MY PLATE. SHE SAY YOU BETTER NO PISS ONNA PLATE, YOU SONNA MA BITCH.

LATER I GO OUT TO EAT AT THE BIGGA RESTAURANT, THE WAITRESS BRINGA ME A SPOON AND KNIFE, BUT NO FOCK. I TELL HER I WANNA FOCK. SHE TELLA ME EVERYONE WANNA FOCK. I TELLA HER YOU NO UNDERSTAND, I WANNA FOCK ON THE TABLE. SHE SAY YOU BETTER NO FOCK ONNA THE TABLE, YOU SONNA MA BITCH.

SO, I GO BACK TO MY ROOM INNA HOTEL AND THERE IS NO SHITS ONNA MY BED. I CALLA THE MANAGER AND TELL HIM I WANNA SHIT. HE TELLA ME GO TO THE TOILET, I SAY, YOU NO UNDERSTAND, I WANNA SHIT ONNA THE BED. HE SAY YOU BETTER NOY SHIT ONNA THE BED. YOU SONNA MA BITCH.

I GO TO THE CHECK OUT AND THE MAN AT THE DESK SAY "PEACE TO YOU" I SAY PISS ONNA YOU TOO, YOU SONNA MA BITCH, I GONNA BACK TO ITALY.

NOTICE

OFFICE OF CIVILIAN DEFENCE
WASHINGTON, D.C.

INSTRUCTIONS TO PATRONS ON PREMISES IN CASE OF NUCLEAR BOMB ATTACK:

UPON THE FIRST WARNING:

1. Stay clear of all windows.

2. Keep hands free of glasses, bottles, cigarettes, etc.

3. Stand away from bar, tables, orchestra, equipment and furniture.

4. Loosen necktie, unbutton coat and any other restrictive clothing.

5. Remove glasses, empty pockets of all sharp objects such as pens, pencils, etc.

6. Immediately upon seeing the brilliant flash of nuclear explosion, bend over and place your head firmly between your legs.

7. Then kiss your ass goodbye.

"LET ME GET THIS STRAIGHT, MY COMPLAINT WAS RELAYED FROM YOUR NIGHT ANSWERING MACHINE TO A COMPUTER WHICH THEN PRINTED OUT MY DATA ON TAPE WHICH WAS THEN TRANSFERRED TO A READER WHICH CORRELATED ALL COMPLAINTS BY AREA AND TYPE, AND THEN – THE CARRIER PIGEON BECAME ILL"?!

THE PLAN

In the beginning was The Plan,

And then came the assumptions,

And the assumptions were without form,

And the plan was completely without substance,

And the Darkness came upon the face of the workers.

And they did rent their garments and spake unto the Production Manager, saying, "Yea, it is an unholy crock of shit and the stench doth offend us".

And the Production Manager went unto the Strategists, saying "It is a pail of excrement and none may abide it's odour thereof".

And the Strategists went unto the Business Manager crying unto the heavens saying "It is a container of manure, it is very strong such that none here may abide it."

And the Business Manager went unto the Director saying unto him,

"Harken unto me, it is a vessel of fertiliser, and none may abide it's strength".

And the Director went unto the Vice-President crying "It contains that which aids plant growth, and is very strong".

And the Vice-President came before the Senior Vice-President and raising his face before God cried loudly "It promoteth growth and it is very powerful – see how we are blessed",

And the Senior Vice-President went forward and spake unto the President saying "Let not your heart be troubled for this new plan will actively promote the growth and efficiency of the company",

And the President looked upon the plan and saw that it was good,

AND LO, THE PLAN BECAME POLICY.

TO: N.O. Way – Senior Engineering Officer

FROM: I.M. Little – Engineering Drawing Dept.

Sir,

My salary review notification arrived today. It came as very much of a shock. As a matter of chance I was in the smallest room of the house when I read your remarks which gave me time to reflect on a response to your memo; I decided to put it behind me.

Yours sincerely

I.M. Little.

GENERAL NOTICE

DATE: 1.4.81
TO: All Staff
FROM: Senior Exec.
REF: SALARY REVIEWS

Signed: M. Grabbit
(Managing Director)

NOTE TO PROSPECTIVE APPLICANTS IN SALES

Those of you scanning the Press for a job in Sales and Marketing had best beware of the applied psychology and sheet dishonesty of some companies. A good marker of what you can expect is given in the phraseology used in their Ads for recruiting sales staff:

1. **'YOUNG DYNAMIC CO.'** – A one man band – he'll be the conductor and you'll play all the instruments.

2. **'SALARY RELATED TO EFFORT'** – Commission only – can you afford it?

3. **'SKY'S THE LIMIT'** – They'll hustle for a sky-high sales target and push you to your limit!

4. **'RAPID PROMOTION'** – Drop-out rate of sales staff is so high that if you survive a week or two you become eligible for the company's debts.

5. **'VIGOROUS AND DEDICATED APPLICANTS BELOW 25 ONLY'** – Low salary and commission – cold calling through the night on trainees' income.

6. **'NO EXPERIENCE NECESSARY'** – Works on probability that out of the 3 or 4 hundred guys they hire (and fire) each week one of them should make a sale.

7. **'PROFESSIONAL WITH PROVEN TRACK RECORD'** – They're poaching – out of the many applicants one will probably have the contacts they want. If you've been selling cars, and they're into paint, forget it!

8. **'FIVE YEARS AGO I WAS PENNILESS – LET ME SHOW YOU HOW TO MAKE £50,000 A YEAR'** – He can't be bright so he must be dishonest. How else do you go from poverty to riches by showing someone else how to become poor?

9. **'MARKET LEADERS – UNIQUE PRODUCT'** – Naturally, who else sells orange flavoured washing-up liquid.

10. **'ALL LEADS SUPPLIED'** – You're cold calling in dog foods and the leads are free gifts.

11. **'CHALLENGING POSITION FOR DEDICATED SALES EXECUTIVE'** – They're operating in a highly competitive market and losing ground – if you are a sales equivalent to a Sherman tank, ruthless, unscrupulous and love to be hated – this could be for you.

"Is this a new advertising slogan Tom, or are you trying to tell us something?"

FIBBER ADVERTISING AGENCY

GUIDELINES FOR ADVERTISERS

1, The truth is what you make it,

so

2, Don't tell lies when you can use statistics.

3, The World is golden unless seen through rose coloured spectacles.

4, The manufacturer has no part in saying what his product can do.

5, Sincerity sells, once you can fake it you can't lose.

6, You can fool 88.75% of the public all the time, the rest haven't got any money.

7, If the product fits into the actresses cleavage, she's not big enough for the job.

8, If the product kills 10% of the market, that still leaves you the remaining 100%.

9, If the product sells, it's due to good advertising exposure, if it doesn't, it's due to bad product design.

FROM: Chief Tech. Officer
TO: Service Manager

Dear Rob

Enclosed with this memo is a letter of complaint from Mr. L.T. Teel.

He's just found out that his V.C.R. is faulty. It's been automatically switching in at the same time every night and re-playing a news broadcast that went out a year ago. He says he couldn't tell the difference until he noticed that the newscaster had been wearing the same tie for the last twelve months.

I know the spares situation isn't all that it should be, so if you can't repair the machine immediately you might think about supplying Mr. Teel with a three hour pre-recorded tape of a test card. Given his previous record, it'll be six months before he realises something's wrong, by which time you can either have the spares in stock or be out of the country.

Regards, Ron.

A WORD FOR ALL SEASONS.

'FUCK'

Our most versatile word – by stress and inflection it can describe many emotions and sentiments. No other word can be used in such varied grammatical nuances. It can be used as a noun (I don't give a fuck), as an adjective (it really is a fucking beauty), as a verb in it's transitive form (the game was fucked by the weather) and the intransitive form (he well and truly fucked up). Everyday expressions show it's genuine versatility;-

Denial	—	*I'll be fucked if I did.*
Perplexity	—	*I know fuck all about it.*
Apathy	—	*Who gives a fuck anyway.*
Greeting	—	*How the fuck are you.*
Goodbye	—	*Fuck off.*
Resignation	—	*Oh fuck it!*
Derision	—	*He fucks everything up.*

The word has, of course, been used by some very famous personages through the years:-

"What the fuck was that?"	— *The Mayor of Hiroshima.*
"Look at all those fucking Indians"	— *General Custer.*
"Where's all that fucking water coming from?"	— *Captain of the Titanic.*
"What a place to plant a fucking tree!"	— *Marc Bolan.*
"There's no fucking mountains near here!"	— *Jim Reeves.*
"That's not a real fucking gun"	— *John Lennon.*
"It looks like a fucking log!"	— *Donald Campbell.*
"Who the fuck will know?"	— *President Nixon.*
"I am outside the fucking exclusion zone!"	— *General Belgrano.*
"Heads are going to fucking roll for this"	— *Anne Boleyn.*
"Any fucker can understand that"	— *Albert Einstein.*
"Watch him, he'll have some fuckers eye out"	— *King Harold.*
"It fucking looks just like her!!"	— *Pablo Picasso.*
"What fucking map?"	— *Mark Thatcher.*

SOFT ENGINEERING CO.

ORDINARY EXAMINATION FOR APPRENTICESHIP CANDIDATES.
Date: Tuesday, 27th June, 1972
(ATTEMPT ALL QUESTIONS) Time Allowed 6 Hours

1. What language is spoken by FRENCHMAN?
2. Give two important characteristics of the ancient Babylonian Empire with particular reference to the architecture, literature and language OR give the first names of the Beatles.
3. What religion is the POPE? Jewish/Catholic/Anglican.

UNDERLINE ONE ONLY.

4. Would you ask WILLIAM SHAKESPEARE to: Build a bridge, Lead an army, Sail an ocean, WRITE A PLAY?
5. What is a Silver Dollar made of?
6. What is the time when the big hand is on the twelve and the little hand is on the ONE?
7. Approximately how many commandments was Moses given?
8. Spell LONDON, DUBLIN, BELFAST, GUINNESS.
9. What country is the Queen of ENGLAND queen of?
10. What are people living in the north of England called? Westerners/Southerners/Easterners/NORTHERNERS/Eskimos.
11. Six Kings of England were called George. The last one was called George VI. Name the other five.
12. Who won World War II. Who came second?
13. Where does rain come from? Supermarkets/U.S.A./ A Big Fountain/THE SKY.
14. Who invented Stephenson's Rocket? Winston Churchill/ Eamonn Andrews/Michael Parkinson/STEPHENSON.
15. Can you explain Einstein's theory of relativity? YES or NO?
16. What is a Coathanger?
17. Who is buried in Thomas Grant's Tomb.
18. At what time is NEWS AT TEN on?
19. Where is the basement in a three storey building?
20. Explain 'Le Chataliers' principal of dynamic equilibrium forces OR write your name in block capitals.

THE IDIOT'S DIGITAL CALCULATOR

COMMUNICATION

1. Read everything before you do anything.

2. Put your name in the upper right-hand corner of the paper, in the space provided.

3. Circle the word "name" in the second sentence, above.

4. Draw five small squares in the upper left-hand corner of this paper.

5. Put an X in each of the five small squares you have drawn.

6. Put a circle around each of those five small squares above.

7. Sign your name, under and to the left of the title above.

8. Draw a circle, in pen, around sentences 6 and 7 above.

9. Multiply 70 x 30 and write the result on the reverse side.

10. Draw a circle around the word "paper" in sentence 4, above.

11. Please now call out your first name, loudly.

12. If you feel that you have carefully followed these directions, call out, loudly: I have carefully followed directions!"

13. Add 107 and 278, and write the sum on the reverse, immediately under the first figure that you wrote there.

14. Circle that figure on the reverse.

15. In a normal voice, count aloud from 1 - 10.

16. If no one else has said it, say now, "I am the leader!".

17. Now that you have read all of the foregoing, very carefully, please complete ONLY sentences 1 and 2.

THE FOLLOWING ARE PURPORTED TO BE ACTUAL STATEMENTS MADE BY CAR DRIVERS IN THEIR REPORTS SUMMARISING THE DETAILS SURROUNDING MOTOR VEHICLE ACCIDENTS. THE DRIVERS WERE ASKED TO DESCRIBE EVENTS IN THE FEWEST POSSIBLE WORDS.

The pedestrian had no idea which direction to run, so I ran over him.

I thought my window was down, but I found out it was up when I put my head through it.

The guy was all over the road, I had to swerve a number of times before I hit him.

Coming home I drove into the wrong house and collided with a tree I don't have.

I was sure the old fellow would never make it to the other side of the road when I struck him.

The other car collided with mine without giving warning of it's intention.

I collided with a stationary truck which was coming the other way.

A truck backed through my windshield into my wife's face.

A pedestrian hit me and went under my car.

I pulled away from the side of the road, glanced at my mother-in-law and headed over the embankment.

In an attempt to kill a fly I drove into a telephone pole.

I had been shopping for plants all day and was on my way home. As I reached an intersection a hedge sprang up, obscuring my vision and I failed to see the other car.

I had been driving for 40 years when I fell asleep at the wheel and had an accident.

I was on my way to the doctor with rear end trouble when my universal joint gave way causing me to have an accident.

As I approached the junction a sign suddenly appeared in a place where no stop sign had ever appeared before.

I was unable to stop in time to avoid an accident.

To avoid hitting the bumper of the car ahead I struck the pedestrian.

My car was legally parked as it backed into the other vehicle.

An invisible car came out of nowhere, struck my car and vanished.

I told the police I was not injured, but on removing my hat found that I had a fractured skull.

I saw a slow moving, sad old gentleman as he bounced off the roof of my car.

The indirect cause of the accident was a little guy in a small car with a big mouth.

I was thrown from my car as it left the road. I was later found in a ditch by some stray cows.

It is said that Traffic Wardens have
YELLOW BANDS on their hats to stop cars
PARKING on their HEADS!

-oOo-

*Say it with FLOWERS, send a TRAFFIC
WARDEN a VENUS FLY – TRAP!*

-oOo-

__THANKS__
FOR PARKING SO CLOSE.
NEXT TIME LEAVE A FUCKING
CAN OPENER
SO I CAN GET MY CAR OUT.
ASSHOLES LIKE YOU
SHOULD TAKE THE BUS!
UP YOURS!

I AM NOT SURE WHAT HE'S DOING.

HE SAYS HE'S FOUND A NEW WAY FOR ME TO
LOSE 7lb OF UGLY FAT!

IF YOU WORK AND DO YOUR BEST,

*YOU'LL GET THE SACK LIKE ALL
THE REST,*

BUT IF YOU LAZE AND BUGGER ABOUT,

YOU'LL LIVE TO SEE THE JOB RIGHT OUT.

THE WORK IS HARD, THE PAY IS SMALL,

SO TAKE YOUR TIME AND SOD'EM ALL,

*COS' WHEN YOU'RE DEAD YOU'LL
BE FORGOT,*

SO DON'T TRY TO DO THE BLOODY LOT –

*FOR ON YOUR TOMBSTONE NEATLY
LACQUERED*

*WILL BE THREE WORDS 'JUST BLEEDING
KNACKERED'.*

"PHILOSOPHER'S CORNER"

SOCIALISM.
*You have two cows
and give one to your neighbour.*

COMMUNISM
*You have two cows;
the government takes both and gives you the milk.*

FASCISM
*You have two cows;
the government takes both and sells you the milk.*

NAZISM
*You have two cows;
the government takes both and shoots you.*

BUREAUCRATISM
*You have two cows;
the government takes both, shoots one,
milks the other and throws the milk away.*

CAPITALISM
*You have two cows;
you sell one and buy a bull.*

JUST BECAUSE YOU'RE PARANOID DOESN'T MEAN THEY AREN'T OUT TO GET YOU.

IF YOU HAVE BLUNDERED,

AND YOU'RE FEELING TWO INCHES TALL,

SEEING A GLOATING FACE LOOKING FROM
    EVERY CORNER,

TAKE HEART,

NO ONE REMEMBERS THE TITANIC'S
    CAPTAIN,

SO WHAT MAKES YOUR BOO-BOO
    MEMORABLE?

(Yes they bloody well do, his name was Captain E.J.Smith!)

ALMOST ANYTHING IS EASIER TO GET INTO THAN OUT OF.

"WELL GENTLEMEN, LET ME WELCOME YOU TO A RATHER EARLY START FOR THE FIFTH DAY OF THIS, THE FIRST INTERNATIONAL SEMINAR ON SLEEP PSYCHOLOGY...."

MEMORANDUM

TO: All Salaried Staff   FROM: The Board

DATE: REF: FK/U

RETIREMENT POLICY

As a result of the reduction of money budgeted for departmental areas, we are forced to cut down on our number of personnel.

Under the plan, older employees will be asked to go on an early retirement, thus permitting the retention of younger people who represent our future plans.

Therefore, a programme to phase out older personnel by the end of the current fiscal year, via retirement, will be placed into effect immediately. The programme will be known as RAPE. (Retire Aged People Early).

Employees who are RAPED will be given the opportunity to look for other jobs outside the company, provided that they are being RAPED, they can request a review of their employment records before actual retirement takes place. This phase of the operation is called SCREW (Survey of Capabilities of Retired Early Workers).

All employees who have been RAPED or SCREWED may file an appeal with upper management. This will be called SHAFT (Study of Higher Authority Following Termination). Under the terms of the new policy employees may be RAPED once, SCREWED twice, but be SHAFTED as many times as the company deems appropriate.

If the employee follows the above procedure he or she will be entitled to get HERPES (Half Earning for Retired Personnel Early Severance). As HERPES is considered a benefit plan, any employee who has received HERPES will no longer be RAPED or SCREWED by the company.

Management wishes to assure the youngest employees who remain on board that the company will continue its policy to ensure that employees are well trained through our Special High Intensity Training (SHIT). The company takes pride in the amount of SHIT our employees receive. We have given our employees more SHIT than any other company in the area. If any employee feels he or she does not receive enough SHIT on the job, see your immediate supervisor. Your supervisor is specially trained to make sure that you receive all the SHIT you can stand.

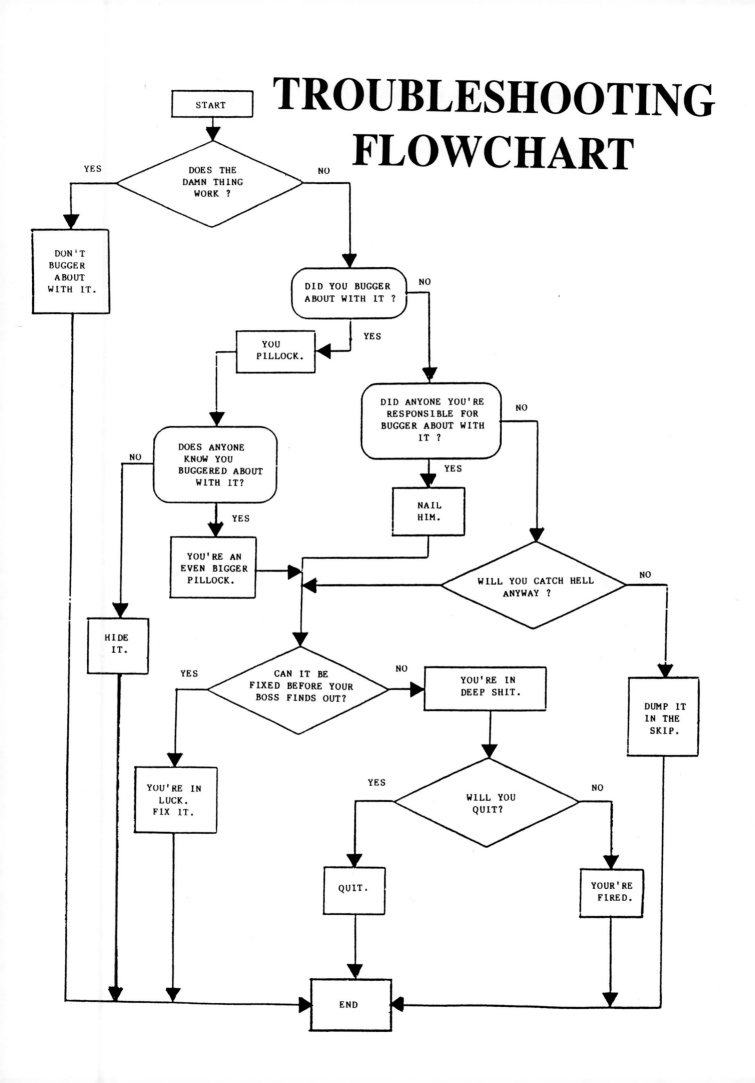

TROUBLESHOOTING FLOWCHART

SELF CERTIFICATION FORM
(OFFICIAL)

APPLICATION TO BE ILL

This form must be submitted at least 21 days before the date on which you wish illness to commence.

NAME .... CLOCK/EMPLOYEE NO ....

DEPARTMENT .... POSITION HELD ....

NATURE OF ILLNESS ....

DATE ON WHICH ILLNESS TO COMMENCE ....

(Applications to suffer from Pregnancy must be submitted 12 months prior, and accompanied by from no. WS.36/24/36. Consent of Husband/Wife ....

HAVE YOU EVER APPLIED TO SUFFER FROM THIS ILLNESS BEFORE ....

IF YES, GIVE DATE ....

DO YOU WISH ILLNESS TO BE SLIGHT/SEVERE/CRIPPLING/FATAL ....

DO YOU WISH TO SUFFER THIS ILLNESS AT HOME/HOSPITAL/COSTA BRAVA/FLORIDA OR BOGNOR REGIS ....

DO YOU WISH THIS ILLNESS TO BE OF A CONTAGIOUS NATURE ....

IF YES, INDICATE APPROXIMATE NUMBER OF PEOPLE YOU WISH TO INFECT ....

HAVE YOU EVER BEEN REFUSED PERMISSION TO SUFFER FROM AN ILLNESS, IF YES, PLEASE GIVE DETAILS ....

DO YOU WISH YOUR WIFE/HUSBAND TO BE INFORMED OF YOUR ILLNESS IF SHE/HE SHOULD CONTACT THE COMPANY REGARDING YOUR WHEREABOUTS ....

I, the undersigned, declare that to the best of my knowledge the answers given above are true and accurate.

Signed .... Date ....

Applicants are reminded that all requests are considered on merit and more than three applications per annum will be considered excessive and not in the best interests of the Company. Under NO CIRCUMSTANCES will permission be given for more than one fatal illness per applicant.

THE SPECIALIST

SOMEONE WHO LEARNS MORE AND MORE,
ABOUT LESS AND LESS, AND ENDS BY
KNOWING ABSOLUTELY EVERYTHING –
ABOUT NOTHING.

Science is merely a collection of abstruse, obscure truths – technology is applied obscurity – that's why you can't understand the operating instructions.

PROTOTYPES GIVE ANSWERS TO QUESTIONS WE DIDN'T KNOW WE SHOULD ASK. AND GIVES THE FALLACY TO ANSWERS WE THOUGHT WE HAD.

THAT'S NOT MY JOB!

This is a story about four people named: Everybody, Somebody, Anybody and Nobody. There was an important job to be done and Everybody was sure that Somebody would do it. Anybody could have done it, but Nobody did it. Somebody got angry about that, because it was Everybody's job. Everybody thought Anybody could do it, but Nobody realised that Everybody wouldn't do it. It ended up that Everybody blamed Somebody when Nobody did what Anybody could have done.

SILENCE!

In this office will be found the finest intellects in the company – undisturbed and left to concentrate, they will navigate the company towards future prosperity. Interruption and loud noises now, could mean your job later. In any case, it plays havoc with one's ability to concentrate on the space invaders and tends to drown out the juke-box.

STAFF CANTEEN

Quite recently, three members of staff were taken to hospital with lockjaw (and in a very astonished state) after they bit into chocolate eclairs which had had the cream replaced with a mixture of silicon rubber and superglue.

Would the person responsible for the 'rubber' incident please contact the canteen staff, since these eclairs are selling better than their own.

> "There is something I don't know that I'm supposed to know,
>
> I don't know what it is I don't know, and yet I am supposed to know;
>
> And I feel I look stupid, if I seem both not to know it and know what it is I don't know...."

The more you study,
The more you see how little you know.
The more you learn,
The less you realise you know.
The less you know –
The more you must study –
The more you study then –
The more you can forget –
(and the less you know!)
The less you actually know,
and the less you realise you know,
The more you must study,
WHY BOTHER!!

IF IT'S SLIMY AND WRIGGLES –
IT'S BIOLOGY.
IF IT SMELLS –
IT'S CHEMISTRY.
IF IT'S INCOMPREHENSIBLE –
IT'S PHYSICS.
IF IT DOESN'T WORK –
IT'S ENGINEERING.
IF IT SHUFFLES ABOUT AND FART'S –
IT'S THE HEAD OF THE FACULTY!

Those who don't study the past will repeat it's errors, those who do study it will find other ways to foul up.

Any event, once it has occurred, can be made to appear inevitable by a competent historian.

"ANOTHER MONTH ENDS"

All Targets Met,

All Systems Working,

All Customers Satisfied,

All Staff Eager and Enthusiastic,

All Pigs Fed and Ready to Fly.

WOULD YOU MIND TERRIBLY IF I ASKED YOU TO TAKE YOUR COCK – EYED, SILLY – ARSED SCHEMES . . NEXT DOOR!

If the chair below is vacant –

I'VE BEEN PAROLED!

BEFORE YOU ASK ME – THE ANSWER IS

NO

TITLES AVAILABLE FROM IDEAS UNLIMITED (PUBLISHING)

Please send me (Postage free)

❑   copies "100 CHAT UP LINES"
ISBN: 1 871964 00 8 (128 pages A7)   @ £1.99

❑   copies "THE IDIOTS' HANDBOOK OF LOVE & SEX"
ISBN: 1 871964 08 3 (128 pages A7)   @ £1.99

❑   copies "WELL HUNG" (Full Colour)
ISBN: 1 871964 07 5 (96 pages A5)   @ £2.99

❑   copies "BODY LANGUAGE SEX SIGNALS"
ISBN: 1 871964 06 7 (64 pages)   @ £2.50

❑   copies "OF COURSE I LOVE YOU"
ISBN: 1 871964 01 6 (96 pages A6)   @ £1.99

❑   copies "THE BEGINNERS GUIDE TO KISSING"
ISBN: 1 871964 02 4 (64 pages A5)   @ £2.50

❑   copies "TIPS FOR A SUCCESSFUL MARRIAGE"
ISBN: 1 871964 03 2 (64 pages A5)   @ £2.50

❑   copies "THE JOY OF FATHERHOOD"
ISBN: 1 871964 04 0 (64 pages A5)   @ £2.50

❑   copies "OFFICE HANKY PANKY"
ISBN: 1 871964 05 9 (64 pages A5)   @ £2.50

❑   copies "10 GOLDEN RULES OF CHATTING UP"
ISBN: 1 871964 09 1 (128 pages A7)   @ £1.99

❑   copies "HAVE YOU SEE THE NOTICE BOARD"
ISBN: 1 871964 10 5   @ £3.99

❑   copies "SPORT FOR THE ELDERLEY" (48 pages)
ISBN: 1 871964 11 3   @ £2.50

I have enclosed a cheque/postal order for £.. made payable to Ideas Unlimited (Publishing).

NAME: ....

ADDRESS ....

....

....

....

COUNTY: .... POST CODE: ....

Fill in the coupon above and send it with your payment to:

Ideas Unlimited (Publishing)
PO Box 125
Portsmouth
Hampshire PO1 4PP

Postage free within the United Kingdom.

If you wish your purchase to be sent directly to someone else (eg: a Birthday / Christmas / Wedding / Valentines gift), simply fill in their name and address in the coupon above and enclose your cheque/postal order, with your personal message or card, if desired. We will be pleased to send your gift directly to your chosen recipient.

DO NOT ADJUST YOUR BRAIN, THERE IS A FAULT IN REALITY.